Sam Choy's
Sampler

Other books by Chef Sam Choy

With Sam Choy
Cooking From The Heart

Sam Choy's Cooking
Island Cuisine At Its Best

The Choy of Seafood
Sam Choy's Pacific Harvest

Sam Choy's Kitchen
Cooking Doesn't Get Any Easier Than This

Sam Choy's Poke
Hawai'i's Soul Food

awai'i is a gourmet 'gathering place' where talented chefs practice their
ft and the festive culinary possibilities are endless." —Chef Sam Choy

Library of Congress Catalog Card
Number: 00-191978

ISBN 1-56647-344-6

First Printing October 2000
Second Printing, November 2000
Third Printing, May 2001
Fourth Printing, March 2002
Fifth Printing, December 2003
Sixth Printing, July 2003
6 7 8 9

Design by Jane Hopkins
All photography by Douglas Peebles except:
    photo on page 1 (background) and 21 (background) by
    Raymond Wong

Mutual Publishing
1215 Center Street, Suite 210
Honolulu, Hawai'i 96816
Ph: (808) 732-1709
Fax: (808) 734-4094
e-mail: mutual@lava.net
www.mutualpublishing.com

Printed in Korea

Sam Choy's
Sampler

Welcome to the Wonderful World
of Hawai'i's Cuisine

by Chef Sam Choy

edited by Joanne Fujita

MUTUAL PUBLISHING

Pronounced po-kay, this favorite island dish is made of seasoned bite-size pieces of raw or seared fish.

Table of Contents

Introduction

Hawaiian cuisine is like a summer soup. You take everything edible out of the refrigerator and cupboard, throw it into a large pot on the stove, and start adding "somma this" and "somma that." Like the story *Stone Soup,* where everybody brought things to add to the pot.

Hawai'i's multicultural society has been putting a big variety of ethnic foods into the Island pot for decades—like the raw fish, fresh seaweed, and tropical fruits of Native Hawaiians; the star anise, fermented black beans, and steamed fish of the Chinese; the sashimi, tofu and teriyaki of the Japanese; the sausages and sweet bread of the Portuguese.

Our cultural mix in the Islands is amazing. Because we have this unique blend of people from all over Asia and Polynesia, the traditional Hawaiian-style cuisine of lū'au food, plate lunches, poke, and bento has evolved to make Hawai'i a gourmet "gathering place," where talented chefs practice their craft and the festive culinary possibilities are endless.

When people come to my restaurant, I want to give them a true taste of the Islands, a real sense of the flavor of Hawai'i. I want every person, whether they're from Hawai'i or elsewhere, to remember the experience. Perhaps one day, six months, a year, or even several years from now, they might be driving somewhere when they smell something and, like a light bulb snapping on in their heads, it'll make them remember the aroma, the taste of something they had eaten at *Sam Choy's.*

That wonderful feeling happens to me—when I go to a tailgate party or to the beach and I smell teriyaki cooking on the hibachi, it takes me back to my childhood, when my dad used to take us to town on Sunday, driving past all the parks. In my mind, I can see the dried squid hanging on the lines; the people standing around in tight, little circles, hooking 'oama by Punalu'u; the local boys surrounding a net for akule outside Kahana Bay. These are memories—of all of this diversity—that are locked in my heart, and will forever inspire me whenever I cook.

This "Sampler" tries to capture the nuances of Hawai'i's famous summer soup—the savory, sumptuous broth filled with "somma the best."

I hope you enjoy it!

Here in Hawaiʻi the lūʻau is the traditional way of celebrating a special occasion.

Sample Menus

Thanksgiving Dinner, Sam Choy Style

Most of the work in this menu can easily be accomplished ahead of time, leaving you with lots of time to enjoy your guests. Prepare the pie, soup and the salad dressing the evening before the party so they will be chilled and ready when you need them. The sweet potato casserole and the turkey bake at the same temperature, so they can share the oven.

Papaya, Mint and Coconut Soup • 20

Organic Field Greens Salad*
with Garlic Ranch Dressing • 35

Kalua-Style Turkey with Dried Fruit
and Oyster Stuffing • 58

Baked Sweet Potatoes • 80

Easy Banana Pie • 98

*Note: Recipes are not given for those items marked with an asterisk, as these are optional dishes that may be changed based on the season and your mood.

A Chic Pacific Rim Dinner

*You can decorate an individual salad plate with a serving each
of the tartare and the shrimp salad for a beautiful presentation. The crusted
ono and the colorful vegetable pasta will look smashing together for
the main course. Be sure to serve a good champagne.*

Summer 'Ahi Tartare • 10

Moloka'i Shrimp Spinach Salad • 30

Crusted Ono as Featured
at Sam Choy's Restaurants • 64

Chinese Pasta Primavera • 83

Pineapple Cheesecake • 92

A Hot Summer Night's Delight

Even though you can cook and chill the chicken ahead of time, make the pesto at the last minute for the best flavor. The dessert is a refreshing frappe for adults.

Hilo Tropical Fruit Slaw • 28

Cold Chicken Tossed
with Fresh Ginger Pesto • 61

Steamed White Rice*

Black Goma Asparagus • 86

Loco Loco Mocha Mocha • 114

Backyard Barbecue

*This low-effort, high-flavor menu will be perfect for a relaxing afternoon
with friends. Have them make their own sandwiches with a selection of fresh
vegetables and condiments. Serve lots of cold beer.*

Pūlehu Tri-Tip, Thinly Sliced • 46

Hibachi Mixed Vegetables • 81

Dinner Rolls or Buns

Tray of Tomato and Onion Slices
and Lettuce Leaves

Condiments

Macadamia Nut Cream Pie • 95

Sunday Night at Grandma's

Local favorites star in this homey menu.

Chicken Salad Chinese-Style
with "Dabest" Sauce • 22

The Best Beef Stew • 44
or Shrimp Curry with Coconut Milk • 77

Steamed White Rice*

Bok Choy Broccoli • 85

Fresh Mangoes with Vanilla Ice Cream*

Fusion Cuisine

*This menu features an international blend of flavors and ideas,
all with a Hawaiian flair.*

Deep-Fried Won Ton Brie
with Pineapple Marmalade • 5

Mixed Green Salad*
with Creamy Oriental Dressing • 32

Oriental Lamb Chops with Rotelli Pasta • 50

Ginger Pineapple Sorbet • 97

Dinner From the Grill

There aren't a lot of things more delicious than chicken roasted over an open fire. Make it memorable with some sweet grilled corn.

Spinach Salad* with Wasabi Vinaigrette • 33

Rotisserie (Huli Huli) Chicken • 60

Garlic Mashed Potatoes • 88

Grilled Corn on the Cob*

Coconut Bread Pudding • 90

Appetizers & Soups

Breakfast Lunch and Crab's Crab Cakes

Deep-Fried Won Ton Brie
with Fresh Pineapple Marmalade

Steamed Clams with Ginger Pesto Butter

Teriyaki Roll-ups

Summer 'Ahi Tartare

Sam Choy's World-Famous Fried Marlin Poke

Da Wife's Bean Soup

Sam Choy's Southpoint Chowder

Papaya, Mint and Coconut Soup

Breakfast, Lunch and Crab's Crab Cakes

I have had so many requests for this recipe since our restaurant in Iwilei opened. I demonstrated it on my KHNL television show, but still there are requests. I decided that putting it in my cookbook was the best way for everyone to get it. So, here it is. Enjoy!

Makes 6 servings

1 pound crab meat
1 dash Worcestershire sauce
1 dash Tabasco sauce
1 tablespoon ogo (optional)
1 teaspoon curry powder
1 teaspoon dry mustard
1 tablespoon scallion, chopped
1 tablespoon red bell pepper, diced
1 teaspoon panko (Japanese crispy bread crumbs) (see "About Panko")
1/4 cup mayonnaise
1 teaspoon Magic Spice Mix (see recipe)
1 cup all-purpose flour
1 cup Clarified Butter (see recipe)
Salt and pepper to taste
Curry Aioli (see recipe)

Remove all shells and cartilage from crab meat. Fold Worcestershire, Tabasco, crab, ogo (optional), curry powder, mustard, scallions, bell pepper, panko, mayonnaise and Magic Spice Mix together. Form into patties, 4 ounces each. Dredge in flour and sauté in Clarified Butter. Arrange crab cakes on platter, and drizzle with Curry Aioli.

Magic Spice Mix

1 teaspoon garlic powder

1 teaspoon onion powder

1 teaspoon Old Bay Seasoning

1 teaspoon paprika

1 teaspoon cayenne powder

Blend.

Curry Aioli

1 cup mayonnaise

1/4 cup fresh cilantro, chopped

1 teaspoon rice vinegar

1 teaspoon fresh lime juice

1 teaspoon curry powder

1 teaspoon sesame oil

Salt and pepper to taste

Blend, and set aside for about 30 minutes.

Clarified Butter

Melt 1 cup butter in microwave oven. Heat for 1-1/2 minutes. Remove, and let set for 20 minutes. Carefully skim to remove the whey.

ABOUT PANKO
Panko are large-flaked, unseasoned dry breadcrumbs. They are available at Japanese markets. You can substitute dry breadcrumbs, though the result may not be as crisp.

Deep-Fried Won Ton Brie with Fresh Pineapple Marmalade

Deep-Fried Won Ton Brie with Fresh Pineapple Marmalade

*Fry the won ton until it is extra crisp.
Bite in and taste the melted brie, combined with
the taste of macadamia nuts. It only gets better
when dipped in homemade marmalade.*

Serving amount varies

Pineapple Marmalade (see recipe on p. 6)
Won ton wrappers
Oil for deep-frying
Brie cheese
Chopped macadamia nuts (optional)
1 egg white

Take a won ton wrapper and brush with egg white.
Place a cube of brie in the middle. (You can add a
sprinkle of chopped macadamia nuts or other nuts if
you like.) Press the cheese down while gathering up
the won ton wrapper to make a little purse, and
pinch the wrapper together just above the cheese to
seal. The won ton wrapper should fan out a little at
the top, with the overall effect being one of a
miniature gift-wrapped package.

In a deep heavy pot or wok, heat oil to 350° F.
Deep-fry purses to a golden brown for about 2 to 3
minutes. Drain on paper towels. Serve with warm
pineapple marmalade.

As an alternate to this method, the brie may be
wrapped in phyllo and baked in a 350° F. oven for
10 minutes or until golden brown.

recipe continued on next page

Pineapple Marmalade

Makes 2 cups

2 cups chopped pineapple (fresh or canned)
I cup granulated sugar
Pinch of hot chili flakes (optional)

In a heavy saucepan, combine pineapple with sugar. Bring the mixture to a boil and then simmer uncovered until it thickens to a syrupy consistency, stirring occasionally. It will take about 45 minutes for fresh pineapple, or less if you're using canned pineapple.

TIP
For a quick dipping sauce, combine a jar of prepared orange or pineapple marmalade and thin with white wine over low heat for about 5 minutes until the sauce becomes a good consistency for dipping. Spice it up with a pinch of hot chili pepper flakes.

Steamed Clams
with Ginger Pesto Butter

When purchasing live clams, make sure all of the shells are closed. If they are open, the clams are dead. Do not eat them. If the clams are frozen, they are sometimes open. If they were previously frozen, and open, it's OK. But if you're buying them fresh, they should all be closed.

Makes 4 servings

24 fresh steamer clams
1 medium round onion, thinly sliced
1/2 teaspoon fresh garlic, chopped
3 cups chicken stock
1 cup fresh shiitake mushrooms, julienned
2 cups mustard cabbage, julienned
1 tablespoon green onion, chopped
Salt and pepper to taste
4 tablespoons Ginger Pesto Butter (see recipe on p. 8)

Rinse fresh clams to ensure that clam shells are closed.

Place clams, onions, garlic, and chicken stock in a small pot. Steam for 1 minute. Add all vegetables, and cook for 2 to 3 minutes. Salt and pepper to taste, then remove from stove.

Divide clams into 4 serving bowls. Dollop each serving with 1 tablespoon Ginger Pesto Butter. Garnish with cilantro leaves, and serve immediately.

Ginger Pesto Butter

4 ounces fresh ginger

1 ounce fresh garlic

1 cup light olive oil

1/4 cup fresh cilantro

1/2 cup green onion

Salt and pepper to taste

1/4 pound butter, softened

Blend all ingredients in a blender.

Teriyaki Roll-Ups

*Island marinade, with papaya, garlic, ginger, soy, brown
sugar and sherry, turns the steak butter tender. Now, roll
it around the vegetables and grill. No barbecue?
A wok will work, too.*

Makes 4 servings

3/4 cup onions, chopped

2 tablespoons fresh garlic, minced

2 tablespoons fresh ginger, peeled and minced

I tablespoon brown sugar

I-1/2 cups soy sauce

I cup water

1/2 papaya, seeded, peeled and mashed

2 tablespoons sherry

I pound flank steak, sliced into thin sheets

2 teaspoons vegetable oil

1/2 cup carrots, julienned

1/2 cup green beans, julienned

2 tablespoons green onions, chopped

1/4 cup red bell peppers, julienned

Salt and pepper to taste

To prepare marinade, combine onions, garlic, ginger,
brown sugar, soy sauce, water, papaya, and sherry in
a large bowl and mix well. Marinate flank steak
overnight in refrigerator.

In a large skillet, sauté remaining vegetables over
medium-high heat until al dente. Lay a thin sheet of
steak on a clean flat surface (like a plate). Spoon
vegetables onto one side of the flank steak, season
with salt and pepper. Roll the meat and secure it with
toothpicks. Grill meat until cooked.

NOTE
Meat rolls can
be grilled in a
large hot skillet,
a wok or over a
hibachi or
barbecue.

Summer 'Ahi Tartare

*When you clean just-caught 'ahi, the bones always have a lot of meat.
Get a big spoon, scoop it out, chop that up and make a fine poke,
like tartare—the best.*

Makes 6 servings

1 pound very fresh 'ahi (yellowfin tuna)

1/4 cup Maui onion, minced

Juice of 1 lemon

2 tablespoons cilantro, chopped

1 tablespoon fresh ginger, minced

1 tablespoon soy sauce

1 teaspoon olive oil

1 teaspoon sesame seed oil

1-1/2 teaspoons fresh horseradish, grated

1/2 teaspoon prepared stone-ground mustard

Pinch red chili pepper flakes

Salt and white pepper to taste

Cut 'ahi into 1-inch cubes.

In a food processor, combine all ingredients and pulse 6 times or until at desired texture. Do not purée mixture. If you don't have a processor, mince 'ahi with a knife into roughly 1/4-inch cubes before combining with other ingredients.

Serve with toast points, crackers or field greens.

Summer 'Ahi Tartare is especially delicious with shiso leaves. This herb, also known as beefsteak plant, can be obtained at Japanese markets. About the size of large basil leaves, they have serrated edges, and come in red or green varieties. They taste like a cross between mint and basil.

NOTE

Only the freshest fish should be used for raw preparations. If you can't obtain 'ahi, choose fish for freshness first. Look for a robustly flavored fish such as a bluefin or skipjack tuna, yellowtail or mackerel.

Sam Choy's World-Famous Fried Marlin Poke

I serve 1,000 pounds of this dish in my Kona restaurant each week, and I'm not kidding when I say it's world famous!

Makes 1 serving

4-6 ounces raw marlin, cut in 3/4-inch cubes
1 teaspoon soy sauce
1/4 cup round onion, chopped
1 teaspoon green onion
1/4 cup ogo seaweed
1 teaspoon sesame oil
1 tablespoon vegetable oil

For each serving, place marlin cubes (if you can't obtain fresh raw marlin, use the freshest raw swordfish or albacore you can find) in mixing bowl with soy sauce, chopped onion and green onion, seaweed and sesame oil. Mix well.

Heat oil in a wok until it's almost smoking, and quickly sear fish. Don't cook for more than a minute or two, as you want the center to be raw.

Serve on a bed of bean sprouts, chopped cabbage, or greens.

ABOUT POKE

Pronounced po-kay, this favorite island dish is made of seasoned bite-size pieces of raw or seared fish. Poke is typically served as a snack or appetizer and is usually seasoned with soy sauce, garlic, seaweed, chili peppers or Hawaiian sea salt. As Hawai'i's many cultures have adopted poke, it has taken many forms—including many varieties of seafood, meats and even tofu. Thanks in large part to the establishment of the Annual Sam Choy Poke Festival, poke has become one of Hawai'i's beloved culinary art forms.

Sam Choy's World-Famous Fried Marlin Poke

Da Wife's Bean Soup

At family gatherings, it's the wife's soup or mine.
My soup always has leftovers, her soup's always gone.
(I think we eat more to make her feel better—just kidding!)

Makes 18 servings

2 cups dried beans (kidney, pinto or small red)
2 smoked ham hocks or ham shanks
3 cups chicken stock
1 cup cilantro, chopped
2 cups potato, diced
2 cups carrots, sliced
1 1/2 cups onion, diced
1/2 cup celery, diced
1 10-oz. Portuguese sausage (see "About Portuguese Sausage")
2 cups tomato purée
Salt and pepper to taste

Soak beans in water overnight. Drain.

In a stockpot, combine soaked beans, ham hocks, chicken stock, cilantro and water to cover (about 6 cups). Bring to a boil, then simmer until meat and beans are tender.

Remove skin and bones from ham hocks; shred meat and return to stock. Slice and fry Portuguese sausage, and blot with paper towel. Add sausage to stockpot along with potatoes, carrots, onion, celery and tomato puree. Cook until potatoes are tender, about 30 minutes. Taste for salt and pepper, and add if necessary.

Goes great with freshly baked bread.

BOUT PORTUGUESE SAUSAGE

rtuguese sausage, also known as linguica, is a popular Hawaiian ingredient. Made
m pork and garlic, it's frequently spiced with chilies. Although other garlic
usages will be successful substitutes for Portuguese sausage, it is worth obtaining
e real thing. Please see the Ingredient Source Guide.

Sam Choy's Southpoint Chowder

As more and more areas around the Hawaiian chain get fished out, we're finding that places like Southpoint on the Big Island, Nihoa on Kaua'i and the windward coasts of every island still harbor an abundance of fish. What is saving those places is the roughness of the weather.

Makes 8 servings

8 mussels
1 pound firm white fish
1/4 pound shrimp
1/4 pound scallops
6 strips bacon, diced
1 onion, minced
3 stalks celery, minced
1 potato, peeled and diced
1 sweet potato, peeled and diced
2 cups Fish Stock (see recipe on p. 18)
1/2 cup creamed corn
1/2 cup fresh corn kernels
Salt and white pepper to taste
Pinch of fresh thyme
2 cups heavy cream
Chopped parsley as a garnish

Rinse mussels and cut in half. Cube fish. Peel and devein shrimp. Set seafood aside.

In a heavy stockpot, fry bacon, onions and celery until onions are translucent. Add potatoes and fish stock. Cover and simmer until potatoes are cooked. Add fish, mussels, shrimp, scallops, salt, white pepper and thyme. Cover and simmer until fish is done. Add creamed corn and corn kernels. Stir in heavy cream and heat thoroughly, but don't boil. Garnish with chopped parsley.

recipe continued on next page

Sam Choy's Southpoint Chowder

Fish Stock

2-1/2 pounds fish bones, rinsed

1 cup white wine

4 stalks celery, chopped

1 carrot, chopped

1 onion, chopped

1 tablespoon fresh ginger, minced

1-1/2 teaspoons sea salt

1/2 teaspoon white pepper

Place fish bones in a large pot. Add white wine, vegetables, ginger, salt, pepper and enough water to cover bones. Bring to a boil. Reduce heat and simmer for 25 minutes. Strain. Fish stock should be used when fresh.

Papaya, Mint and Coconut Soup

Nothing like a cool soup on a hot Hawaiian day.
Ripe papayas and coconut milk make this rich and creamy.
You can leave out the rum when the kids are eating.

Makes 4 servings

2 medium-sized ripe papayas, peeled, seeded and chopped
2 cups coconut milk
2 tablespoons dark rum (optional)
2 tablespoons mint leaves
2 teaspoons honey
1 teaspoon island seasoning (nutmeg, cinnamon, thyme and allspice)

Garnish:
Sprigs of mint

Place the papayas, coconut milk, rum (optional), mint leaves, honey and island seasoning in a food processor. Purée for 20 to 30 seconds or until mixture is smooth. Refrigerate 1 hour before serving. Garnish each serving with a sprig of mint.

NOTE
If you'd like to try your hand at making fresh coconut milk, see p. 78 for instructions.

Salads

Chicken Salad Chinese-Style
with "Dabest" Sauce

Lasagna-Style Hibachi Tofu Salad

Hilo Tropical Fruit Slaw

Moloka'i Shrimp Spinach Salad

Sam's Signature Salad Dressings

Chicken Salad Chinese-Style with "Dabest" Sauce

The jumbo shrimp give this classic Chinese Chicken Salad a gourmet touch. Cook the shrimp just enough. If you cook them too much, they won't be tender. Black and white sesame seeds and chopped green onions give "dabest" sauce a festive look.

Makes 4 servings

"Dabest" Sauce (see recipe)
2 pounds skinless, boneless chicken thighs
Salt to taste (for boiling water)
1 pound extra jumbo shrimp (16 to 20), peeled and deveined
1 medium iceberg lettuce cut into thin strips
2 stalks celery, cut in round slices
1 medium cucumber, seeded, halved lengthwise and sliced horizontally
1 green bell pepper, julienned
1 small Napa cabbage, thinly sliced
2 medium carrots, julienned

Garnish:
Won ton chips or fried won ton wrapper strips (see Note)

Place rinsed chicken in a pot and cover with salted water. Bring water to a simmer and boil chicken for 30 to 45 minutes. Remove chicken from pot and cool slightly. Refrigerate until completely cooled.

When chicken is cool, bring 3 inches of water to a boil in a large saucepan. Add shrimp to liquid. As soon as water returns to a boil, remove shrimp. Do not overcook.

In a large bowl, add shrimp, iceberg lettuce, celery, cucumber, green bell pepper, Napa cabbage, carrots and cooled chicken. Add sauce and won ton strips to salad ingredients and lightly toss. Serve immediately.

"Dabest" Sauce

Makes 1-1/2 cups

1/4 cup granulated sugar

3/8 cup rice vinegar

2 teaspoons salt

1/2 cup salad oil

2 tablespoons white sesame seeds, lightly toasted

1 tablespoon fresh ginger, peeled and minced

3 tablespoons green onions, chopped

1 tablespoon soy sauce

1 teaspoon black sesame seeds

Whisk together sugar, vinegar and salt until sugar and salt are dissolved. Gradually add salad oil while continually whisking until all oil is incorporated. Add remaining ingredients and mix well.

NOTE
If using won ton wrappers, cut 12 pieces into thin strips. Fry in a small pot of oil heated to 375° F. Drain on paper towels.

Lasagna-Style Hibachi Tofu Salad

▲▽//▲▽//▲▽//▲▽//▲▽//▲▽//▲▽//▲▽//▲▽//▲▽//▲▽//▲▽//▲

*Stacking the tofu gives this salad a unique look.
The hibachi grill gives it a unique flavor; the Creamy Oriental Dressing
and Ginger Pesto make the flavor double good.*

Makes 2 servings

Lasagna-Style Hibachi Tofu Salad Marinade (see recipe on p. 26)
Creamy Oriental Dressing and Wasabi Vinaigrette (see recipes on p. 32-33)
20 ounces firm tofu
4 tablespoons olive oil
1/2 cup zucchini, julienned
1/2 cup sweet onions, julienned
1/2 cup carrots, julienned
1/2 cup red bell peppers, julienned
1/2 cup yellow bell peppers, julienned
1/2 cup bean sprouts
1/2 cup shiitake mushrooms, sliced
Salt and pepper to taste
1 to 2 handfuls of rinsed spring mixed greens

Garnish:
Ginger Pesto (see recipe on p. 27)

Drain tofu and slice the whole block lengthwise into four equal sections.
Marinate for 1 to 2 hours.

Prepare coals in hibachi.

In wok or sauté pan, heat olive oil until very hot, but not smoking. Add
julienned vegetables, bean sprouts, and mushrooms. Stir-fry for 2 to 3
minutes or until vegetables are just wilted. Season with salt and pepper.

recipe continued on next page

Lasagna-Style Hibachi Tofu Salad

Add a handful or two of spring mixed greens and remove quickly from wok.

Remove tofu from marinade, cook on hibachi over hot coals (2 to 3 minutes on each side), and then remove from heat.

To serve, place a small amount of stir-fried vegetables on salad plate, place 1 slice of tofu on top of vegetables, put a layer of vegetables on tofu, and continue alternating tofu and vegetables until you finish with a layer of vegetables on top. Garnish with Ginger Pesto and drizzle dressing over each layer, either Creamy Oriental or Wasabi Vinaigrette, or both.

Lasagna-Style Hibachi Tofu Salad Marinade

Makes 2 cups

2 cloves garlic, minced
1-1/2 cups soy sauce
1 cup granulated sugar
1/4 cup fresh ginger, peeled and minced
2 tablespoons green onions, thinly sliced
1 tablespoon fresh cilantro
1 teaspoon sesame oil
1/8 teaspoon white pepper

Combine ingredients and mix until sugar is dissolved.

Ginger Pesto

Makes about 1-3/4 cups

1/4 cup fresh ginger, peeled and minced
1/2 cup green onions, chopped
8 garlic cloves (about 1 ounce), peeled
1/4 cup fresh cilantro
1 cup salad oil
Salt and pepper to taste

Combine ginger, green onions, garlic, cilantro and salt and pepper in a food processor and purée for 15 seconds. With the processor running, pour salad oil slowly through the feeding tube in a steady stream. When well blended, this can be used immediately or refrigerated for later use.

Hilo Tropical Fruit Slaw

At the Hilo Open Market you can see all the fresh fruits.
So I brought out a file recipe and created a slaw using the fruits.
This is ideal with broiled chicken breast.

Makes 8 (1-cup) servings

Hilo Tropical Fruit Slaw Dressing (see recipe below)
1 papaya, seeded, peeled and thinly sliced
1 cup fresh pineapple, peeled and thinly sliced
1 medium mango, peeled and thinly sliced
1 star fruit, ribs trimmed, thinly sliced and seeded
1 kiwi fruit, peeled and thinly sliced
6 strawberries, hulled and quartered
1/2 cup whole poha berries (cape gooseberries)
1 banana, sliced
1 medium head radicchio, leaves separated

In a large salad bowl, combine fruits and fold in prepared dressing. Serve on radicchio leaves.

Hilo Tropical Fruit Slaw Dressing

1 ripe papaya, seeded and peeled
2 tablespoons honey
1/2 cup plain yogurt
1/4 teaspoon each salt and white pepper

Machine process dressing ingredients 30 seconds. Makes 2 cups.

Hilo Tropical Fruit Slaw

Moloka'i Shrimp Spinach Salad

This recipe has one of just about every Island flavor.
The secret is in the layering of texture and tastes. Taking the time to
oven-roast the bell pepper is well worth the effort.

Makes 4 servings

Shrimp Marinade (see recipe on p. 31)
Warm Spinach Salad Vinaigrette (see Recipe on p. 31)
1 pound jumbo shrimp (16 to 20 count) peeled and deveined
4 cups fresh spinach, rinsed and dried

Garnish
1 oven-roasted bell pepper, sliced (see Note)
2 eggs, hard boiled and diced
1 tablespoon macadamia nuts, minced

Marinate shrimp for 30 minutes. Then, fry in a wok on high heat and set aside.

Pour Warm Spinach Salad Vinaigrette over spinach leaves and toss. On individual plates, layer with spinach, shrimp, eggs, bell pepper slices and macadamia nuts.

Shrimp Marinade

Makes 1-1/4 cups

1 cup soy sauce
2 tablespoons brown sugar
1 tablespoon fresh garlic, minced
2 teaspoons red chili pepper flakes
1 tablespoon fresh cilantro, minced
1 tablespoon fresh ginger, peeled and minced
1/4 teaspoon white pepper
1/2 teaspoon sesame seeds

Combine.

Warm Spinach Salad Vinaigrette

Makes 3/4 cup

1/2 cup pine nuts
2 tablespoons balsamic vinegar
2 tablespoons fresh lemon juice
2 tablespoons granulated sugar
1/2 teaspoon cracked peppercorn
1/4 teaspoon sesame seeds
1/4 teaspoon red chili pepper flakes

In a wok, stir vinaigrette ingredients together over medium-high heat until warm.

NOTE
To prepare bell peppers for roasting, wash and remove seeds and ribs of pepper membranes. Place cleaned peppers on baking pan. Char peppers under broiler until the skin blisters. Make sure to carefully turn pepper to make sure all sides blister. Place pepper in tightly sealed brown paper bag for 20 minutes, then peel off loosened skin with a knife.

Sam's Signature Salad Dressings

The thing about these dressings is that they are good enough to just eat with a spoon. Each one has a "best use" but that shouldn't stop you from trying them on whatever strikes your fancy. They work with salad, seafood, pasta and even as sandwich spreads and dips.

Creamy Oriental Dressing

Makes 4 cups

3 cups mayonnaise
1/2 cup soy sauce
3/4 cup granulated sugar
1/4 teaspoon white pepper
1-1/2 tablespoons black sesame seeds
1 tablespoon sesame oil

Whisk all of the ingredients together until well blended. If the consistency is too thick, whisk in a few drops of water at a time, until you get the consistency you desire.

Wasabi Vinaigrette

*Certain salads need spicing up to reach their peak.
Wasabi adds a whole different flavor. I knew it was real
popular with sushi and sashimi. So I wanted to play with
it in a vinaigrette where people would notice it and
have it wake up their taste buds, but where it
wouldn't be overpowering.*

Makes 3 cups

2 cups freshly squeezed orange juice
2 tablespoons sesame seeds
3 tablespoons granulated sugar
1/2 cup canola oil
3 tablespoons vinegar
2 tablespoons soy sauce
Salt to taste
2 tablespoons wasabi powder

Combine ingredients and mix together until well
blended.

Sam's Special Thousand Island

*Thousand Island dressing is very basic and easy to make.
To make it unique, tofu and hard-boiled eggs are added to give the dressing
a texture, almost as if the dressing is a salad in itself. This dressing can
turn a simple salad into something very special.*

Makes 3-1/2 cups

2 cups mayonnaise

1/2 cup half and half

4 teaspoons sweet pickle relish, drained

4 tablespoons chili sauce

1/2 tablespoon black sesame seeds

1/2 teaspoon dried red chili pepper flakes

White pepper to taste

2 hard-boiled eggs, chopped

1/2 cup tofu, diced

Combine mayonnaise, half and half, pickle relish, chili sauce, sesame
seeds, and chili flakes; mix well. Gently fold in tofu and chopped eggs.

Garlic Ranch Dressing

This dressing is creamy and rich and makes eating salads a very memorable experience. I love to use garlic in my cooking because it spices up and brings out the flavor of whatever you put in on. Ranch dressing is very versatile. It can be used for salads, sandwiches, and dips as well.

Makes 4 cups

3 cloves garlic, minced

1/2 cup onions, minced

1/4 cup granulated sugar

1/4 cup red wine vinegar

1/2 cup olive oil

2 cups mayonnaise

Salt and pepper to taste

2 teaspoons dry mustard

1 tablespoon fresh oregano, minced

1 tablespoon fresh basil, chopped

Combine all ingredients and whisk until thoroughly blended. Chill.

Sweet and Sour Cucumber Vinaigrette

*This vinaigrette was inspired by a simple Asian dipping sauce.
By adding a few more ingredients, this vinaigrette goes well on salad,
crispy won ton or spring rolls and with spicy lamb or poached fish.*

Makes about 3 cups

1 cup white vinegar

1/2 cup water

3/4 cup granulated sugar

1 cup cucumbers, very thinly sliced

1/2 tablespoon fresh ginger, peeled and grated

Pinch of salt

White pepper to taste

Combine all ingredients and blend until sugar dissolves. Chill.

Meats

Easy Local Ribs

Local Style Veal Osso Buco
with Shiitake Mushrooms

The Best Beef Stew

Hawaiian Pūlehu Tri-Tip Steak

Sweet and Sour Pineapple Pork

Oriental Lamb Chops with Rotelli Pasta

Easy Local Ribs

Oven braise a local favorite—sweet and sour spareribs packed with pineapple.

Makes 4 servings

3 pounds meaty country-style pork spareribs, cut in pieces

3 tablespoons soy sauce

1 teaspoon salt

Dash pepper

Pineapple chunks

Green onions, chopped

Sauce:

1 cup syrup-packed pineapple chunks, drained

1/2 cup packed brown sugar

1/3 cup ketchup

1/3 cup vinegar

2 tablespoons soy sauce

2 teaspoons fresh ginger, grated

2 cloves garlic, minced

Rub spareribs all over with 3 tablespoons of the soy sauce, salt and pepper. Place ribs, meat side up, in a foil-lined shallow baking or roasting pan, and cover with foil or baking-pan lid. Bake 20 to 25 minutes at 450° F. Drain off fat.

Combine sauce ingredients; pour over ribs. Bake at 350° F for 1 hour or until tender, basting occasionally.

Garnish with pineapple chunks and green onions.

Easy Local Ribs

Local Style Veal Osso Buco with Shiitake Mushrooms

It's natural when you hear the phrase "osso buco" to automatically think Italian, but what we're doing here is taking the osso buco cut of veal and poaching it oriental style, then saucing it with the rich broth and shiitake mushrooms.

Makes 4 servings

4 veal shanks, cut about 1-1/2 inch thick
Salt and pepper to taste
1/2 cup flour for dusting meat
3 tablespoons oil
4 cloves garlic, crushed
1/4 cup carrots, coarsely chopped
1/2 cup onions, coarsely chopped
3 tablespoons Chinese parsley
1 tablespoon five spice powder
1/2 cup soy sauce
Enough chicken broth or stock to cover meat
1 cup sugar
1/2 cup sherry
Shiitake Sauce

Sprinkle veal shanks with salt and pepper, dust with flour, then brown in 3 tablespoons oil in large braising pan for 1 to 2 minutes per side. Add garlic, carrots, onion, Chinese parsley, five spice powder and soy sauce. Brown it all together for another 5 minutes. Cover with chicken broth or stock. Bring to a boil and add sugar and sherry. Cover with foil or ovenproof lid and braise in 350° F oven for 1 hour, or until tender. Reserve cooked broth for Shiitake Sauce. Keep veal warm while preparing sauce. Pour sauce over veal to serve.

recipe continued on next page

Local Style Veal Osso Buco with Shiitake Mushrooms

Shiitake Sauce

3 tablespoons oil

1/2 cup sweet red and yellow bell peppers, julienned

1/2 cup onions, julienned

1/4 to 1/2 pound snow peas

1 cup shiitake mushrooms, sliced

3 cups strained stock from braised veal

4 tablespoons cornstarch mixed with 3 tablespoons water

To make sauce, heat oil on medium-high heat in large sauté pan or wok and stir-fry vegetables 2 to 3 minutes. Add strained stock from braised veal, bring to a boil and thicken with cornstarch mixture.

The Best Beef Stew

The Best Beef Stew

*The natural flavors of the vegetables and the beef
really shine through in this classic dish. The surprise combo of beef stock
and chicken stock give the gravy a smooth, long simmered taste.*

Makes 6 servings

4 pounds chuck roast
Salt and pepper to taste
All-purpose flour to dust meat (about 1 cup)
1/2 cup salad oil
2 cloves garlic, crushed
1 small onion, minced
1/2 cup celery leaves, chopped
5 cups beef stock or low-sodium broth
2 cups chicken broth
1-1/2 cups tomato paste
3 medium carrots, cut in 1-1/2" chunks
4 potatoes, cut in 1-1/2" chunks
2 medium onions, cut in 1-1/2" chunks
4 stalks celery, cut in 1-1/2" chunks
Mochiko (sweet rice flour) and water to thicken (see "About Mochiko")

Cut beef into bite-size pieces and sprinkle with salt and pepper. Dust beef with flour.

In a large pot, heat oil over medium heat and brown meat with garlic, onion and celery leaves for about 10 minutes or until well browned. Keep stirring to avoid burning.

Drain oil and add beef and chicken broth and tomato paste. Stir and bring mixture to a boil, then reduce heat to simmer. Cover and let cook about 1 hour, or until beef is tender.

Add carrots and potatoes and cook 5 minutes. Add onion chunks and celery and cook 10 minutes more. Adjust seasoning with salt and pepper.

Mix mochiko and water into a thick syrup. Bring stew to a boil and add mochiko mixture a little at a time, simmering and stirring until you get the right consistency. Remove from heat and refrigerate overnight. Flavors in this stew are best if given a chance to blend.

ABOUT MOCHIKO

Mochiko is a glutinous rice powder with a high starch content. If you can't obtain mochiko, you may substitute cornstarch.

Hawaiian Pūlehu Tri-Tip Steak

*Crusty on the outside and rare on the inside.
That's the secret to this mouth-watering dish. It could almost be
called beef sashimi. Hot is wonderful, but cold sandwiches the next
day allow the flavors to mature very nicely, thank you.*

2-1/2 pounds tri-tip steak (triangular tip of the sirloin)
1/2 cup sea salt
1 tablespoon fresh garlic, minced
1/2 tablespoon cracked peppercorns
1 tablespoon granulated sugar

Prepare your charcoal for grilling.

Rub salt, garlic, pepper, and sugar into the meat and let sit 30 minutes.
Pūlehu in Hawaiian means "to broil on hot embers" and that's what you
do, turning the meat every 4 minutes until done. Total cooking time is
about 10 to 15 minutes, depending on the thickness of the cut.

Sweet and Sour Pineapple Pork

*This is a real local dish with a heavy Asian influence,
as well as a distinctive Hawaiian touch. Coming as I do from the hills of
Wahiawa on O'ahu's north shore, I'd often drive past fields of pineapple and
see all the pickers out there working, but I never gave it much thought until
1968, when I went to work for eight weeks in a Lāna'i pineapple field.
When you see the pickers out there working it looks easy,
but man, it's really hard work.*

Makes 4 servings

1 pound lean pork
1 tablespoon soy sauce
1 tablespoon sweet vermouth
1 teaspoon garlic, minced
1 teaspoon ginger, minced
2 tablespoons vegetable oil
1/2 cup cornstarch
4 cups oil for deep-frying
2 tablespoons vegetable oil
1/2 cup red and yellow bell pepper, diced
2 tablespoons onion, diced
Sweet and Sour Sauce (see recipe on p. 49)
Strips of green onion, for garnish
Toasted sesame seeds, for garnish

Cut pork into bit-size pieces and marinate for 30 minutes in mixture of
soy sauce, vermouth, garlic, ginger and 2 tablespoons oil. Set aside.
Meanwhile, make the Sweet and Sour Sauce as directed in recipe.

Remove pork pieces from marinade and roll in cornstarch to coat well.
Deep fry in 330° to 350° F oil until golden brown and crispy.

In a large sauté pan, heat 2 tablespoons oil on medium-high heat. Stir-fry bell peppers and diced onion for 2 minutes, then add Sweet and Sour Sauce and fold in fried pork. Let simmer 2 minutes, arrange on serving platter and garnish with long strips of green onion and toasted sesame seeds.

Sweet and Sour Sauce

1/2 cup tomato ketchup

1/2 cup vinegar

1/2 cup water

2 teaspoons soy sauce

1 cup sugar

1/4 cup orange marmalade

1-1/2 teaspoons ginger, minced

1 teaspoon garlic, minced

1/4 teaspoon hot pepper sauce

2 tablespoons pineapple juice

1/2 cup canned pineapple, chopped

**4 tablespoons cornstarch mixed with 3 tablespoons
    water**

In a medium saucepan combine all ingredients except cornstarch mixture, blend well and bring to a boil. Add cornstarch mixture. Reduce heat and simmer, stirring frequently, until thickened. Be sure and bring your sauce to a boil before adding the cornstarch, otherwise the sauce may retain an unpleasant starchy taste. (The amount of cornstarch in my recipes is just a suggestion; you may want to add more for a thicker sauce. But be careful. A little cornstarch goes a long way.)

Oriental Lamb Chops
with Rotelli Pasta

One of the most popular dishes in the Sam Choy restaurants, this recipe combines the Italian with the Asian. The pasta, drenched in the cream sauce, makes the perfect bed for the marinated chops.

Makes 4 to 6 servings

Creamy Rotelli Pasta (see recipe on p. 52)
1/2 cup soy sauce
3/4 cup fresh garlic, minced
1 tablespoon fresh ginger, peeled and minced
2 cups brown sugar
1/2 teaspoon red chili pepper flakes
1/2 cup fresh basil, minced
1/2 cup fresh cilantro, minced
Salt to taste
8 to 12 lamb chops (2 to 3 per person)

Combine soy sauce, garlic, ginger, brown sugar, chili pepper, basil, cilantro and salt. Massage into meat for 5 to 10 minutes, then let marinate 4 to 6 hours in refrigerator.

Prepare Rotelli Pasta as directed (see p. 52). Heat broiler and broil chops to the doneness of your liking. (Broil for 2 to 3 minutes per side for medium rare.) Serve 2 or 3 chops over each serving of pasta.

recipe continued on next page

Creamy Rotelli Pasta

Makes 4 servings

2 tablespoons butter
4 tablespoon olive oil
1-1/2 tablespoons fresh garlic, minced
1 medium carrot, julienned
2 medium zucchini, julienned
2 cups shiitake mushrooms, julienned
2 cups cilantro, coarsely chopped
12 ounces rotelli pasta
1-1/2 cups heavy cream
Salt and pepper to taste
3/4 cup Parmesan cheese, grated

Cook pasta a bit firmer than usual, drain and set aside.

In a large saucepan, heat butter and olive oil over medium-high heat. Sauté garlic for about 1 minute. Add vegetables and stir-fry for 2 to 3 minutes. Add drained pasta and stir-fry for another minute. Add heavy cream, bring to a boil and immediately reduce to a simmer. Adjust seasoning with salt and pepper. Just before serving, add Parmesan cheese and let cook 1 minute.

Poultry

Chicken and Coconut Milk

Sam Choy's Award -Winning Roast Duck

Kalua-Style Turkey with Dried Fruit and Oyster
Stuffing and Baked Sweet Potatoes

Rotisserie (Huli Huli) Chicken

Cold Chicken Tossed with Fresh Ginger Pesto

Chicken and Coconut Milk

Canned spinach can be used, along with canned coconut milk.
Any cut of chicken may be used as long as it's boneless. This is a quick
Hawaiian favorite that can look as if you cooked all day.

Makes 6 servings

2 pounds boneless, skinless chicken
2 cups coconut milk
1 quart low-sodium chicken broth
2 cups steamed spinach (see note)
Salt to taste

Cut chicken into 2-inch pieces, place in a pot and cover with chicken broth. Simmer over low heat for 10 to 15 minutes. Add coconut milk and cook for 30 minutes or until tender. Add the cooked and drained spinach; salt to taste and simmer for 5 minutes.

NOTE
2 cups canned or frozen spinach may be used in place of 2 cups steamed fresh spinach. If you'd like to try your hand at making fresh coconut milk, see page 78.

Sam Choy's Award-Winning Roast Duck

Sam Choy's Award-Winning Roast Duck

This "people's award" winning dish is much easier than it seems. A traditional Chinese roast duck takes lots of time. This simple short-cut recipe offers all the taste in half the time.

Makes 4 to 6 servings

2 ducks (3 to 4 pounds each)
3/4 cup soy sauce
I tablespoon salt
I tablespoon garlic salt
I teaspoon garlic powder
I teaspoon paprika
1/2 teaspoon white pepper
I tablespoon coriander seeds (whole)

Remove wing tips, neck flap, tail end, excess fat and drumstick knuckles. Rinse both ducks. Place in a dish, and pour soy sauce over them. Roll the ducks in the soy sauce and let sit for about 20 minutes. Keep rolling in the soy sauce every 3 to 4 minutes.

Preheat oven to 550° F.

Mix remaining ingredients to make a dry marinade. Place duck breast right side up on rack in a roasting pan and sprinkle thoroughly with marinade. Also, put a little marinade inside cavities.

Roast for 30 minutes. Reduce heat to 325° F. Cook for 1 hour or until meat thermometer registers an internal temperature of 170° to 175° F. No basting is necessary.

Serve with steamed rice.

Kalua-Style Turkey with Dried Fruit and Oyster Stuffing and Baked Sweet Potatoes

*No need to dig up the front lawn, this kalua turkey
does just fine in the oven. The stuffing is "Sam special." Serve it with
the baked sweet potatoes and you have a real holiday feast.*

Dried Fruit and Oyster Stuffing (see recipe on p. 59)

Baked Sweet Potatoes (see recipe on page 70)

1 whole turkey with giblets (about 15 pounds)

Hawaiian salt to taste

1/4 cup soy sauce

2 tablespoons liquid smoke

2 quarts chicken stock or low-sodium chicken broth

10 medium size ti leaves (see note)

Preheat oven to 350° F.

Wash turkey, pat dry inside and out. Rub with soy sauce and season
generously with salt and pepper. Place half the ti leaves in a roasting pan,
add liquid smoke and chicken stock to the pan, add the turkey, breast
down, to the pan and cover with remaining ti leaves. Seal pan very well
with foil. Bake for about 4 hours or until done (depending on turkey
size). After turkey cools, shred the meat off the bone.

Dried Fruit and Oyster Stuffing

Begin with bacon for flavor and for the great aroma of the bacon and the onions cooking in the pan. Add several dried fruits. Cranberries add the festive look. The oysters should be poached a bit then added in. The sweet bread gives 'ono flavor.

Makes about 8 cups

1/4 pound bacon, chopped

1/4 cup onion, chopped

1/4 cup carrots, chopped

1/4 cup celery, chopped

1/4 cup garlic cloves, peeled

1/4 cup thyme leaves, stripped from stems

Turkey giblets, chopped

1 pound assorted dried fruit (cranberries, mangoes, papayas)

1 quart chicken stock or low-sodium chicken broth

1 quart oyster meat in juice

2 cups toasted Hawaiian sweet bread cubes (about 1/2-inch pieces)

Salt and pepper to taste

Render the bacon and sauté the onion, carrots, celery, garlic and thyme. When vegetables are cooked, add the giblets and dried fruits. Cook for 5 minutes. Add the chicken stock and oysters (lightly poach oyster meat in juice before adding to stock). When hot, add the sweet bread (for a drier stuffing, add less stock). Cook until all the liquid is absorbed, and season with salt and pepper to taste.

NOTE
If you can't obtain ti leaves, you may use banana leaves, though they will add a slightly different flavor. (The leaves are not to be eaten.) You can safely omit the leaves, just seal very well with foil.

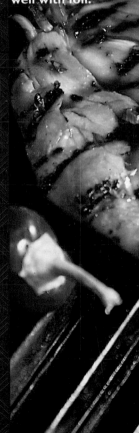

Rotisserie (Huli Huli) Chicken

*In Hawaiian, "huli" means to turn, and "huli huli" means
to turn over and over, and that's just what you do
in cooking this Island favorite.*

2 frying chickens (2 to 3 pounds each)
4 tablespoons salad oil
1 tablespoon garlic, minced
1 tablespoon salt
1/2 teaspoon paprika
1 teaspoon coriander seeds, crushed
1/2 teaspoon black pepper

Split each chicken down the backbone, but leave attached at the breast.
Remove neck bone. Rub chickens with oil and garlic and let sit for 30
minutes. Mix remaining ingredients and sprinkle on chickens so that
they are seasoned very well. Secure on rotisserie and roast 45 minutes to
1 hour. Basting is not necessary.

If you don't have a rotisserie, you can grill on a hibachi for the same
amount of time, turning every 10 to 15 minutes, or broil in your oven,
45 minutes to 1 hour, turning with the same frequency.

If you don't feel like turning it, you can bake it in your oven at 350° F,
breast side up.

Cold Chicken Tossed with Fresh Ginger Pesto

Ginger pesto and chicken make a perfect marriage of flavors. How can you beat that? It's fresh-tasting. Every bite just explodes with flavor.

Makes 6 servings

2 cups water
1/2 cup cilantro, chopped
1-inch piece ginger, crushed
Fresh Ginger Pesto (see recipe on p. 62)
2 cloves garlic, minced
1/2 teaspoon salt
6 skinless, boneless chicken breast halves

In a medium pot, bring to a boil the water, cilantro, ginger, garlic and salt. Add chicken, reduce heat, then simmer 6 minutes or until tender. Remove chicken from water and chill. Cut chicken in 1-inch wide strips and toss with Fresh Ginger Pesto. Great with crisp assorted greens in a salad or with hot steamed rice.

recipe continued on next page

Fresh Ginger Pesto

Makes 1 cup

1/2 cup canola oil
1/2 teaspoon salt
1/4 cup fresh ginger, minced
1/4 cup green onion, minced
1/4 cup lightly packed cilantro, minced
1/2 cup macadamia nuts, finely chopped
2 tablespoons shallots, minced
1/8 teaspoon white pepper

In a small saucepan, heat oil and salt 2-3 minutes; cool. Stir in remaining pesto ingredients.

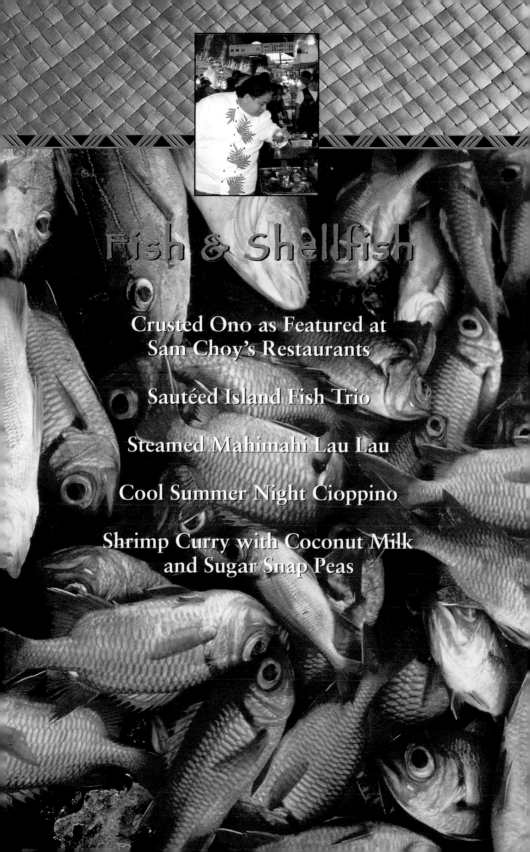

Fish & Shellfish

Crusted Ono as Featured at
Sam Choy's Restaurants

Sautéed Island Fish Trio

Steamed Mahimahi Lau Lau

Cool Summer Night Cioppino

Shrimp Curry with Coconut Milk
and Sugar Snap Peas

Crusted Ono as Featured at Sam Choy's Restaurants

▲▼▲▼▲▼▲▼▲▼▲▼▲▼▲▼▲▼▲▼▲▼▲▼▲▼▲▼

Crusted ono is one of the bestsellers. It has a kind of reputation, but it works. People love it. It's very good, very good.

Makes 4 servings

4 ono (wahoo) fillets (6 ounces each)
1/4 cup olive oil
1 teaspoon fresh ginger, minced
1 teaspoon garlic, minced
Salt and pepper to taste
1/2 cup Ritz Cracker crumbs
1/2 cup butter at room temperature
1/4 cup macadamia nuts, chopped
1 tablespoon fresh herbs, minced (combination of basil, dill & thyme)
1 teaspoon paprika
Papaya-Mango Salsa (see recipe on p. 66)

Marinate ono in mixture of olive oil, ginger, garlic, salt and pepper.

Preheat oven to 375° F. Combine cracker crumbs, butter, macadamia nuts, herbs and paprika; blend well. Divide cracker-crumb mixture into 4 portions and pat 1 portion on top of each fillet. Bake 8 to 10 minutes.

Serve with Papaya-Mango Salsa.

recipe continued on next page

Papaya-Mango Salsa
Makes 2-1/2 cups

3 tablespoons sugar
1-1/2 tablespoons vinegar
Pinch red chili pepper flakes
Pinch cumin
1 medium papaya, seeded, peeled and diced
1 cup mango, peeled and diced
1/2 small red onion, diced
3 tablespoons red bell pepper, diced
2 tablespoons cilantro, chopped

Mix sugar, vinegar, chili flakes and cumin until sugar dissolves. Fold in remaining ingredients.

NOTE
If ono cannot be obtained, substitute an equal portion of any firm white-fleshed fish.

Sautéed Island Fish Trio

Sautéed Island Fish Trio

*Mahi, 'ahi and 'opakapaka are favorites. Separate, they are delicious.
Put them together and they present a flavor combination made in heaven.
The cream and mushroom sauce surrounds them in a lush, rich pool. If you
can't obtain these fish, try for any three contrasting types of fish: one
that is dark and robust—like tuna, one that is moist and sweet—
like snapper, and one that is firm and lean—like halibut.*

Makes 4 servings

Trio Sauce (see recipe on p. 69)
5 cups vegetables, julienned (see Note)
3 tablespoons butter
3 tablespoons olive oil
1/2 teaspoon garlic, minced
Salt and pepper to taste
4 (2-ounce fillets) 'opakapaka (pink snapper)
4 (2-ounce fillets) mahimahi
2 (2-ounce fillets) 'ahi (yellowfin tuna)
1/2 cup flour to dust fish

Garnish:
4 sprigs of fresh parsley or sprigs of your favorite fresh herbs

Heat 2 tablespoons butter and 1 tablespoon olive oil and sauté
vegetables and garlic for 2 minutes. Season with salt and pepper.
Remove from pan, set aside and keep warm.

Lightly season fish with salt and pepper and dust with flour. Heat 3
tablespoons butter and 2 tablespoons olive oil in large sauté pan. Cook
fish until medium-rare, about 1-1/2 minutes per side.

Divide vegetables into 4 equal portions and mound 1 portion in the middle of each plate. Arrange 1 plate filled with each of the three different types of fish around the side of the vegetable mound in a sort of pyramid fashion. Pour sauce around the edge and garnish with a sprig of parsley or other fresh herb.

Trio Sauce
Makes 1 to 2 cups

1 tablespoon soy sauce
2 cups heavy cream
1 tablespoon ginger, minced
1 cup shiitake mushrooms, sliced
Salt and pepper to taste

In pan, combine cream and mushrooms. Bring to a boil, then reduce heat to a low simmer. Add ginger, soy sauce, salt and pepper. Simmer for another 3 to 4 minutes, or until the sauce is reduced to the consistency you like. Keep warm.

NOTE
Use a combination of your favorite stir-fry vegetables such as bell peppers (assorted colors), zucchini, carrots, string beans, snow peas or asparagus.

Steamed Mahimahi Lau Lau

*Using a steaming method is a good way to cook this moist, delicate fish.
It helps retain the moisture, texture, and fresh flavor of this great-tasting, mild
white fish. If you can't obtain mahimahi, try this recipe with a flavorful
white-fleshed fish like halibut or pompano.*

Makes 4 servings

2 cups carrots, finely julienned
2 cups zucchini, finely julienned
1 cup shiitake mushrooms, sliced
8 ti leaves (see "About Ti Leaves")
12 fresh mahimahi fillets (2 ounces each)
Salt and pepper to taste
Enough string to tie each lau lau

Herb Sauce:
1-1/2 cups mayonnaise
1 tablespoon soy sauce
1 tablespoon fresh dill, chopped

Mix carrots and zucchini together and divide into 4 equal portions.
Divide mushrooms into 4 equal portions. Mix herb sauce ingredients
and set aside. Remove hard rib from ti leaves to make flexible, or cook
leaves on high in microwave oven for 1 minute to soften.

To build each lau lau, first make a ti leaf cross on the table by laying 1 ti
leaf over another at right angles. Sprinkle vegetable mix in the center,
then lay a mahimahi fillet on top of vegetables. Spread a thin layer of
herb sauce on fish and sprinkle with more vegetables. Place another fillet
on top, spread with herb sauce, and sprinkle with vegetables. Finish with
a third fillet that is topped with herb sauce, vegetable mix, and a
sprinkle of mushrooms. Season with salt and pepper to taste.

recipe continued on next page

Steamed Mahimahi Lau Lau

Gather up ti leaves to make a purse around fish and tie tightly with string just above bundle. Repeat for all four portions, using a fourth of the vegetables, a fourth of the mushrooms and three mahimahi fillets for each lau lau. Steam for 8 to 10 minutes.

ABOUT TI LEAVES

Ti leaves are from a woody plant of the agave family, Cordyline australis. Used extensively in Polynesia as a wrap for food, they function much like corn husks do in making tamales. Ti leaves contribute their distinctive flavor to the foods they wrap, so it's worth making an effort to use them. If ti leaves are unavailable, wrap the lau lau in parchment paper instead, making bundles by tying the loose edges of paper above the ingredients in a topknot.

Cool Summer Night Cioppino

Cool Summer Night Cioppino

*Cool summer nights call for a seafood cioppino,
which is basically the kitchen sink in a pot. You dip the scoop in
and heaven knows what you're going to bring up.*

Makes 12 servings

1-1/4 pounds firm white fish (yellowfin tuna, mahimahi or wahoo)

2-1/2 cups fat-free chicken stock

2 cups clam juice

1/4 cup olive oil

1 tablespoon garlic, minced

1 Maui (sweet) onion, thinly sliced

1 cup celery, thinly sliced

1 cup red bell pepper, julienned

1 large fresh tomato, diced

1 pound shrimp (about 21 to 25)

1/4 pound clams or mussels, shells scrubbed and rinsed

1 cup white wine

1 cup fresh basil, chopped

1 Hawaiian chili pepper, seeded and chopped (or 1/4 teaspoon red chili
   pepper flakes)

Pinch saffron

1 spiny lobster (1 pound), cleaned and cut in half

Salt and pepper to taste

Cut fish in 1-inch cubes.

In a large pot, combine chicken stock, clam juice and wine; bring to boil.

In another large pot, heat oil and sauté garlic, onion, celery, bell pepper and tomato 2 to 3 minutes—adding fish, shrimp and clams. Add wine and cook 2 minutes more. Add hot stock, basil, chili pepper, saffron and lobster. Adjust seasoning with salt and pepper. Cook 8 minutes or until lobster is done.

Shrimp Curry with Coconut Milk and Sugar Snap Peas

This is my kids' favorite. My wife cooks it, I cook it, the kids love it. I think a lot of other people also love it. The secret is—don't overcook the shrimp.

Makes 6 servings

1 pound extra-large shrimp (about 16 to 20), peeled and deveined
6 tablespoons butter
2 tablespoons olive oil
1 small onion, finely chopped
1 tablespoon curry powder
1 teaspoon sugar
1/2 teaspoon fresh ginger, minced
1/2 teaspoon salt
Pepper to taste
1/4 cup flour
2 cups heavy cream
1 cup chicken stock
1/2 cup coconut milk (see "About Coconut Milk")
2 cups fresh sugar snap peas, blanched

In a heavy skillet, heat 2 tablespoons of the butter and olive oil, and sauté onion and curry powder until onion is translucent. Add shrimp, sugar, ginger, salt and pepper. Sauté 3 or 4 minutes, then remove to a plate.

recipe continued on next page

In the skillet, melt remaining 4 tablespoons butter, stir in flour and cook 5 minutes. Slowly add cream, chicken stock and coconut milk, stirring constantly until mixture is smooth and thick. Return shrimp to pan, along with snap peas; heat through. Serve with steamed rice.

ABOUT COCONUT MILK

Allow yourself to make fresh coconut milk. It's definitely a winner. The process is not hard with the juicers available today.

You can buy already husked coconuts at the market. Use a hammer to crack a coconut. Use a butter knife to dig out the coconut meat. Cut the coconut meat into small strips. Drop the coconut strips into a juicer and extract the milk. Strain the coconut milk through cheesecloth. Dilute the thick and rich coconut milk by adding 1/2 cup water to 1 cup fresh coconut milk; then add to a favorite recipe.

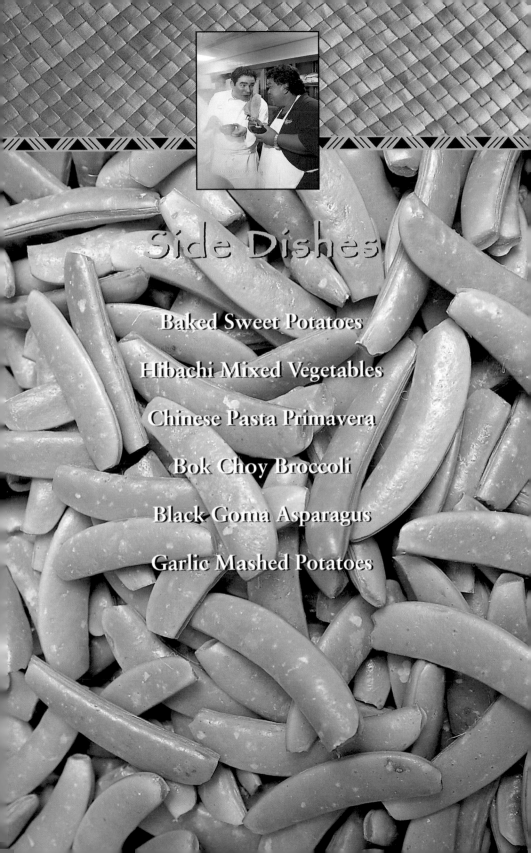

Side Dishes

Baked Sweet Potatoes

Hibachi Mixed Vegetables

Chinese Pasta Primavera

Bok Choy Broccoli

Black Goma Asparagus

Garlic Mashed Potatoes

Baked Sweet Potatoes

This dish is good any time of year. Butter the pan, dot the sweet potatoes with more butter. Add raisins, more butter, macadamia nuts and more butter. Drizzle with coconut syrup and add just a bit more butter!

Makes 12 cups

1 pound butter

6 pounds sweet potatoes, pre-cooked and thinly sliced

1/2 cup packed brown sugar

1 cup raisins

Salt and pepper to taste

1/2 cup all-purpose flour

1/2 cup macadamia nuts, chopped

4 ounces coconut syrup

Preheat oven to 350° F. Rub a casserole dish with butter and spread the sweet potato slices in. Dot with butter, brown sugar, raisins, salt and pepper. Bake for 40 minutes. When done, combine the flour, macadamia nuts, remaining butter and coconut syrup until it is dry and resembles crumbly pie dough. Top the casserole with the macadamia mixture and bake until it is golden brown, 30 to 40 minutes.

NOTE:
This dish bakes at the same temperature as the Kalua Turkey, so it can share the oven.

Hibachi Mixed Vegetables

The variety of colors in this side dish makes it pretty for the plate. The secret here is the 30-minute multi-spiced marinade. Once these tasty vegetables come off the hibachi they won't be on that plate long.

Makes 4 servings

Mixed Vegetable Marinade (see recipe below)
2 cups zucchini, oval sliced
2 cups yellow squash, oval sliced
I cup red bell pepper, sliced
8 rinsed and quartered fresh shiitake mushrooms

Mix sliced vegetables with marinade for 30 minutes.

Prepare coals in a hibachi (or barbecue grill). Cook vegetables over hibachi until done.

Mixed Vegetable Marinade
Makes 1/3 cup

I teaspoon fresh garlic, chopped
1/4 teaspoon black pepper
1/4 teaspoon chili sauce
I teaspoon fresh cilantro, chopped
I teaspoon thyme leaves
I tablespoon white wine
I tablespoon salad oil
I teaspoon sesame oil
1/4 teaspoon soy sauce
1/4 teaspoon oyster sauce

Mix all ingredients together.

NOTE
To prevent vegetables from falling into the coals, use a grid or grilling mesh. This will make barbecuing small items like vegetables and fish a lot easier.

Chinese Pasta Primavera

Chinese Pasta Primavera

*Pasta is trendy and classic. It can seem very Asian
and very Italian at the same time. The more sautéed
vegetables you toss in a bowl of fresh-cooked pasta, the
more the mouth waters. Add snow peas and Thai basil
and you're in Asia. Add a bit of Parmesan
and you can be in Italy, too.*

Makes 8 servings

1 pound dry linguine
1 medium red bell pepper, cut into strips
1 medium yellow bell pepper, cut into strips
2 medium zucchini, trimmed but not peeled, sliced
1/2 pound broccoli florets
1/2 pound asparagus, cut in 1-inch pieces
1/2 pound sugar snap or Chinese snow peas
6 shallots or green onions, sliced very thin
1 clove garlic, minced
1 tablespoon butter
1 tablespoon olive oil
1/4 cup fresh cilantro, chopped
2 tablespoons fresh Thai basil, chopped
Salt and pepper to taste
1 tablespoon soy sauce
1/4 cup Parmesan cheese, freshly grated

Fill a large pot with water and begin heating it for
the pasta.

In a large skillet or wok, heat oil and butter and stir-
fry vegetables, onion, and garlic about 3 minutes.
Add cilantro and basil and cook another minute, or

recipe continued on next page

until vegetables are done to your taste (they should be a little crunchy). Season vegetables with salt and pepper and mix with soy sauce.

When the water boils, add linguine and cook al dente according to package directions. Drain. Toss vegetables with pasta and sprinkle with Parmesan cheese.

Bok Choy Broccoli

Makes 6 servings

2 tablespoons cooking oil

1 medium onion, thinly sliced

1 tablespoon fresh ginger root, grated or minced

2 cloves garlic, crushed

1/2 teaspoon salt

3 cups fresh broccoli florets, sliced

1 pound bok choy, coarsely chopped

2 tablespoons lemon juice

1-1/2 teaspoons sugar

1 tablespoon soy sauce

Heat oil in wok or skillet on medium-high heat until it's almost smoking. Add onion, ginger, garlic and salt. Stir-fry for 2 minutes. Add broccoli and bok choy and stir-fry for 1 minute. Add lemon juice, sugar and soy sauce and stir-fry for 3 minutes, or until crisp-tender.

Black Goma Asparagus

Makes 4 servings

1 pound asparagus
3 slices fresh ginger
1/4 cup chicken broth
1 tablespoon soy sauce
1/2 teaspoon sugar
2 tablespoons vegetable oil
1/2 teaspoon salt
1 teaspoon black goma (black sesame seeds)

Wash asparagus, break off tough ends and discard. Cut stalks diagonally in 1-1/2-inch sections. If the asparagus is young and tender, blanch stalks (but not tips) by immersing quickly in boiling water and rinsing immediately under cold water. Mature asparagus should be parboiled in salted water for a minute or two, removed as soon as it begins to turn bright green, and rinsed immediately in cold water and drained. Do not blanch or parboil the tips.

Mince or crush the ginger. Combine broth, soy sauce and sugar. Heat the oil on medium-high and, when it's almost smoking, add the salt and ginger and stir-fry a few seconds. Add asparagus and stir-fry until heated through. You may have to adjust the heat to prevent scorching.

Add broth mixture and heat quickly. Simmer, covered, over medium heat for 2 to 3 minutes. Sprinkle with black sesame seeds and serve.

Black Goma Asparagus

Garlic Mashed Potatoes

Makes 4 servings

2-1/4 pounds potatoes
4 whole cloves garlic
1/2 pound butter
3 ounces cream
White pepper and salt, to taste

Peel and cut the potatoes into 1-inch cubes.

In a pot, cover the potatoes with cold water, add garlic and bring to a boil. Cook for 8 to 10 minutes, or until done. Drain. Purée in a food processor or whip with an electric mixer. Add the butter and cream. Season with salt and white pepper. Serve immediately.

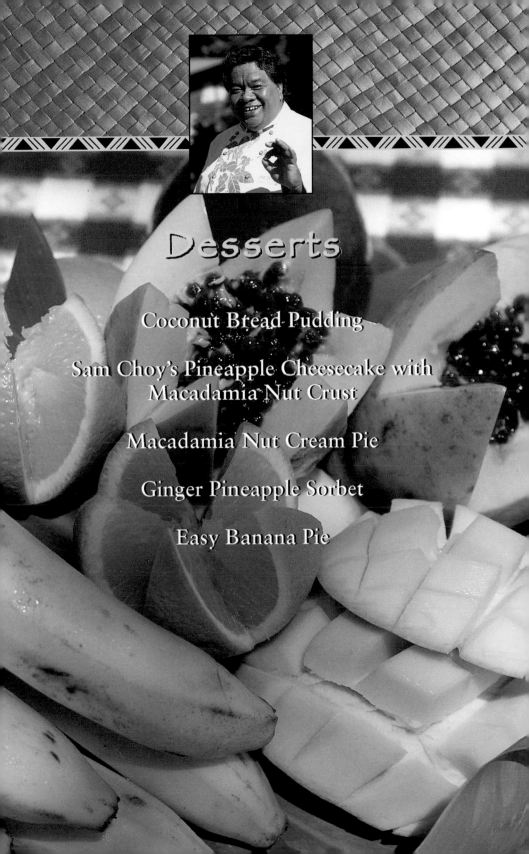

Desserts

Coconut Bread Pudding

Sam Choy's Pineapple Cheesecake with
Macadamia Nut Crust

Macadamia Nut Cream Pie

Ginger Pineapple Sorbet

Easy Banana Pie

Coconut Bread Pudding

Coconut Bread Pudding is a staple dessert at my Breakfast Lunch and Crab restaurant in Iwilei. We top it with a scoop of ice cream (sometimes vanilla, sometimes coconut). If you want to test this dessert out before you make it, come on down.

Makes 8 servings

3 eggs
3/4 cup granulated sugar
4 cups milk
6 tablespoons coconut milk
8 cups bread, diced (about 1/2-inch cubes)
1/2 cup toasted macadamia nuts, chopped
1/2 cup toasted coconut flakes

Garnish (Per Serving)
2 tablespoons coconut syrup
Toasted macadamia nuts, chopped
Toasted coconut flakes
Pineapple, diced
Whipped cream

Whisk eggs and sugar together. Add milk and coconut milk, and mix thoroughly.

Layer bread, macadamia nuts, and coconut flakes in 9 x 13-inch pan. Pour custard mixture evenly over top, and let custard soak into bread. Bake at 325° F for 45 minutes to 1 hour, until a toothpick inserted into the center comes out clean.

When serving, drizzle about 2 tablespoons of coconut
syrup over each portion. Top with a swirl of whipped
cream. Sprinkle with diced pineapple, macadamia
nuts and coconut flakes.

Sam Choy's Pineapple Cheesecake with Macadamia Nut Crust

▲▼▲▼▲▼▲▼▲▼▲▼▲▼▲▼▲▼▲▼▲▼▲▼▲▼▲▼▲

*We are currently serving this very popular pineapple cheesecake
at my Diamond Head restaurant. The candy-nut crust sets off the creamy
cheese filling. Serve each piece on a bed of Créme Anglaise, with colorful fresh
fruits, i.e. strawberries, raspberries, blackberries, kiwi. Enjoy!*

Makes 8 servings

Macadamia Nut Crust
1 cup macadamia nuts
1/2 cup granulated sugar
3 tablespoons sweet butter, melted

Chop the macadamia nuts in a food processor to coarse-meal
consistency, but not so fine that the oil from the nuts makes them sticky.
Combine the sugar with the nuts. Stream in the butter while mixing.

Cheesecake Filling

3-1/2 8-ounce packages of cream cheese
1-1/4 cups granulated sugar
Pinch of orange zest (optional)
Pinch of lemon zest (optional)
1/4 cup heavy cream
1-1/2 cups sour cream
4 large eggs
1 pineapple, diced small

Soften the cream cheese, sugar and zest together in a power mixer or
food processor. Add the cream, sour cream and eggs one ingredient at a
time, mixing well, and scraping the bowl down before adding the next
ingredient.

Caramel Sauce

2-1/2 cups granulated sugar
1 cup water
1 tablespoon lemon juice
3 cups cream

Make caramel from sugar, water, and lemon juice, and remove from heat. Scald the cream. Slowly add cream to the caramel. Bring back to boil just enough to melt all the sugar.

Assembly and Baking:
Preheat oven to 350° F. Grease the cake pan and lay a circle of parchment or waxed paper on the bottom. Pack the crust in the bottom of the pan and bake for 5 to 10 minutes until very lightly brown. In a towel, squeeze some of the juice out of the pineapple. Pour half the batter on top of the pre-baked crust. Stir the pineapple into the rest of the batter. Pour the rest of the batter into the cake pan, and smooth the top.

Using a squeeze bottle, take 1/2 cup of the caramel sauce and swirl on top of the cake batter. To achieve more of a marbled effect, take the tip of the knife and gently swirl the caramel into the batter. Bake in a water bath for 1 hour and 15 minutes to 1-1/2 hours. Test with a skewer or paring knife to see if the cake is done. Let cool, and then chill for at least 3 hours.

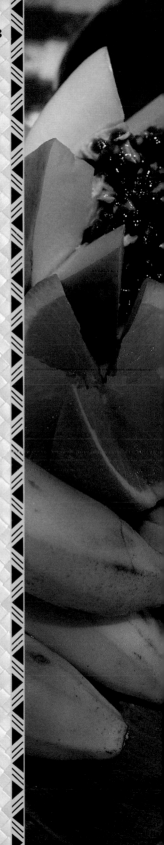

Macadamia Nut Cream Pie

Macadamia Nut Cream Pie

*Living in the Kona district of the Big Island gives
me great opportunities to create dishes using premium
macadamia nuts. I pick the best of the crop, and use
them in my recipes and restaurants.*

Makes 8 servings

3 egg yolks

3 cups milk

3/4 cup granulated sugar

1/3 cup cornstarch

1/4 teaspoon salt

2 tablespoons butter

1-1/2 teaspoons vanilla extract

1 cup macadamia nuts, roasted and chopped

1 9-inch baked pie shell

Garnish:
Whipped cream
Macadamia nuts, coarsely chopped

Combine egg yolks, milk, sugar, cornstarch, salt, and
butter. Bring to a boil over medium heat, stirring
constantly. Boil for 1 minute, and remove from heat.
Stir in vanilla and macadamia nuts. Pour into pie
shell, and chill covered with plastic wrap.

When firm, garnish pie with whipped cream and
macadamia nuts

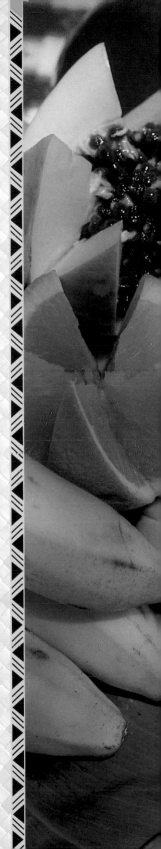

Ginger Pineapple Sorbet

Ginger Pineapple Sorbet

Makes 6 servings

1 cup sugar
1/2 cup pineapple juice
1 tablespoon fresh lemon or orange juice
1 tablespoon fresh ginger, grated
1 pint cream

Mix ingredients. Place in freezer until partially frozen, then put in a bowl and mix well with a wooden spoon. Return to freezer until frozen.

Easy Banana Pie

Makes 8 servings

1 8-ounce package cream cheese, softened
1 cup dairy sour cream
3 tablespoons sugar
3 cups bananas, sliced, dipped in lime or lemon juice
Graham Cracker Crust (see recipe below)
Whipped cream

Blend cream cheese and sour cream. Add sugar and mix well. Add bananas.

Pour into graham cracker crust. Freeze until firm. Remove from freezer 5 minutes before serving. Top with whipped cream.

Graham Cracker Crust

1 cup fine graham cracker crumbs
2 tablespoons sugar
3 tablespoons butter or margarine, melted

Combine ingredients and press firmly into an unbuttered 9-inch pie pan by pressing down with another pie pan. Chill until firm, about 45 minutes.

A Traditional Lūʻau

Traditional Lomi Lomi Salmon

No-Imu Kalua Pig

My Mom's Squid Lūʻau

Poi

Straight Hawaiian-Style ʻInamona Poke

Chicken Long Rice

Pineapple Haupia

The Lūʻau—
Celebrating Hawaiian Style

Here in Hawaiʻi the lūʻau is the traditional way of celebrating a special occasion. On any given weekend, you will find lūʻau going on all over. They are held for birthdays, anniversaries, weddings, grand openings of new businesses, blessings of boats, the opening or closing of a sports or cultural event, and for any other reason someone feels like celebrating. And we're not talking pupu or crackers and cheese—this is heavy eating, true feasting.

It's a tradition in Hawaiʻi to hold a baby lūʻau on your child's first birthday, as a way of giving thanks that your baby made it through the first year, because in the old days lots of babies didn't make it to their first birthday. Anywhere from 50 to 5,000 people will show up for one of these baby lūʻau, and it's real festive, with Hawaiian entertainment and endless food, and it can go on for two or three days. I learned to cook as a kid helping my dad cater lūʻau in Laie.

Planning a Menu for a Lūʻau

I've included only a few of my favorite lūʻau recipes here; a big lūʻau will have many additional dishes. Although it is recommended that you retain some traditional dishes, you may add or substitute any dishes that have the right festive feel. The idea is to have fun. Here are some other dishes in this book that will be appropriate for a lūʻau:

Sam Choy's World-Famous Fried Marlin Poke
Hilo Tropical Fruit Slaw
Hawaiian Pūlehu Tri-Tip Steak
Chicken and Coconut Milk
Rotisserie (Huli Huli) Chicken
Any Recipe From the Dessert Section
Any Recipe From the Tropical Drink Section

Dressing for a Lūʻau

Lūʻau are always casual events that are best enjoyed outdoors at the beach or poolside. Aloha-wear such as aloha shirts and muʻumuʻu are designed for comfort (with lots of room for real feasting!) so they will always be the best bet. Otherwise, have your guests dress as they would for a barbecue. Flower lei are one of the best traditions from Hawaiʻi, and if the budget allows, it's a beautiful gesture to give a lei to each guest. Shell lei are an inexpensive alternative. The proper method of giving a lei is to accompany it with a hug and a kiss.

Setting the Scene

Tropical flowers and plants, Hawaiian music and props such as fishing nets, outrigger paddles and sea shells will go a long way in setting the tone for your party. You might also consider decorating the bathroom your guests will use so it will be consistent with the theme. Have your friends and family help you decorate—it's the sense of togetherness that makes a lūʻau special!

Traditional Lomi Lomi Salmon

Traditional Lomi Lomi Salmon

Makes 24 servings

4 cups salted salmon, diced

12 ripe tomatoes, diced

4 small red onions, diced

1 cup green onion, thinly sliced

1-2 Hawaiian chili peppers, or 1/4 teaspoon red pepper
   flakes (optional)

Combine all ingredients and mix well. Serve well
chilled.

NOTE

Salted salmon comes in various degrees of saltiness,
so it's a good idea to taste it before making this dish.
If it's too salty, you need to soak it overnight in
enough water to cover, and then rinse it twice before
using.

No–Imu Kalua Pig

The traditional way to cook a whole pig Hawaiian style is in an underground oven, or imu. It's a lot of work and it takes all day, but man, does it taste good. Lots of people still do it this way for parties and special events, but you can also do it in your oven with a lot less hassle, and it tastes almost as good.

Makes 24 servings

8 pounds pork butt

4 tablespoons liquid smoke

4 tablespoons Hawaiian salt

8-12 large ti leaves, ribs removed (see "About Ti Leaves")

Preheat oven to 350° F. After scoring pork an all sides with 1/4-inch deep slits about an inch apart, rub with salt, then liquid smoke. Wrap the pork completely in ti leaves, tie with string, and wrap in foil.

Place meat in a shallow roasting pan with 2 cups water and roast for 4 hours.

Dissolve 1 tablespoon Hawaiian salt in 2 cups boiling water and add a few drops of liquid smoke. Shred the cooked pork and let stand in this solution for a few minutes before serving.

ABOUT TI LEAVES

Ti leaves come from a woody plant of the agave family, *Cordyline australis*. They are used extensively in Polynesia as a wrap for food. In this recipe, they are not necessary for the success of this dish. But if you can obtain them, they will add an authentic flavor to your kalua pig.

My Mom's Squid Lū'au

Makes 12 servings

2 pounds calamari

3 pounds lū'au leaves (see "About Lū'au Leaves")

1 tablespoon Hawaiian salt

1/2 teaspoon baking soda

6 tablespoons butter

2 medium onions, diced

3 cups coconut milk

1-1/2 teaspoons salt

1 tablespoon sugar

Clean calamari and slice in rings, then set aside.

Wash lū'au leaves, and remove stems and thick veins. In a pot boil 3 cups of water with the Hawaiian salt and baking soda. Add the leaves to the boiling water and reduce heat. Simmer, partially covered, for 1 hour. Drain, and squeeze out liquid.

Sauté onions and calamari in butter until the onions are translucent. Add the coconut milk, cooked lū'au leaves, salt and sugar. Simmer for 30 minutes.

ABOUT LU'AU LEAVES

Lū'au leaves, which are the leaves from the taro plant, are very high in oxalic acid. Simmering them for an hour is necessary to make them safe to eat. Do not reduce the cooking time for this step. Baking soda also serves to neutralize the acid.

Spinach may be substituted for the lū'au leaves, though the consistency and flavor of the dish will be a little different. You can omit the baking soda and quickly blanch or steam the spinach and use it for the recipe. Be sure to squeeze out excess moisture before adding it to the coconut milk.

My Mom's Squid Lū'au

POI

You must have poi with your lūʻau whether you like it or not. It just isn't a lūʻau without it. Poi has been a Hawaiian staple for thousands of years. It is very nutritious and good for you, and if you sample it often enough, you will eventually acquire a taste for it—maybe. If you're not used to it, it's best to eat it when it's very fresh, although some people like it better after it has sat around for a few days and becomes sour.

I don't recommend making poi yourself, as it's a lot of work and very time-consuming, and you can't beat the commercial variety. If you live outside of Hawaiʻi, please see the Ingredient Resource Guide for ways of purchasing poi.

Commercial poi comes in various forms, the most popular being the type sold in plastic bags. All you need to do to get the poi ready to eat is to add a third-cup or so of water to the bag, seal the top and mix by kneading the bag. When the poi is smooth, pour it out into individual serving bowls.
If you're feeling ambitious, you can try making poi from scratch.

Poi—From Scratch

Makes 12 servings

3 pounds taro corms, peeled, boiled and diced into 1-inch cubes
3 cups water

Mash boiled taro in a wooden bowl with a wooden potato masher until you've turned it into a thick paste. Little by little, work in the water with your hands, then force the poi through several layers of cheesecloth to remove lumps and fiber.

Serve it fresh, or let it ferment for that distinctive sour taste by allowing it to stand for 2 to 3 days in a cool place.

Straight Hawaiian-Style 'Inamona Poke

*Taste of old—this recipe is simple, straightforward.
It definitely brings back a lot of memories of my old days
picking limu (seaweed) from certain parts of the
ocean and Hukilau Bay.*

Makes 12 (1/4-cup) servings

1 pound very fresh raw aku (skipjack tuna), 'ahi
   (yellowfin tuna) or other fish, cut in bite-size cubes
1 small ball limu kohu (edible red seaweed, about 1/2
   cup, chopped)
'Inamona (roasted, crushed, kukui nut, about 1
   teaspoon to taste) (see "About 'Inamona and Limu
   Kohu")
1 Hawaiian red chili pepper, minced
Salt to taste

Rinse and chop limu kohu. In a mixing bowl,
combine all ingredients.

ABOUT 'INAMONA AND LIMU KOHU

These two traditional Hawaiian ingredients may be a
bit hard to obtain outside of Hawai'i. Fortunately, the
World Wide Web is proving to be a good source, even
for obscure items like these. It is strongly
recommended that you obtain the limu kohu for this
recipe (see Ingredient Source Guide), as there isn't a
good substitute for this ingredient.
'Inamona is a condiment made of salted kukui nuts
(candlenuts). You can substitute 1-1/2 teaspoons
cashew nuts, roasted, crushed and salted for the
quantity of 'inamona in this recipe.
Limu Kohu is a fine-textured red seaweed
(*Asparagopsis taxiformis*) that adds a faint iodine scent
to the dishes it flavors.

Straight Hawaiian-Style ʻInamona Poke

Chicken Long Rice

This is an acquired taste. Kids joke that it looks like worms. Once you savor the dish with the chicken and shredded vegetables, accompanied by some fresh poi, green onions and Hawaiian salt, you will never pass it by again, no matter what the kids say!

Makes 12 servings

4 ounces long rice (see "About Long Rice")
20 dried shiitake mushrooms
4 cups chicken broth
2 pounds skinless boneless chicken, cubed
2-inch finger of fresh ginger, crushed
1 medium onion, minced
2 cups celery, thinly sliced
2 carrots, julienned
6 green onions, cut in 1-inch lengths

Soak long rice in warm water for 1 hour. Soak mushrooms in warm water for 20 minutes and drain. Remove stems and slice caps.

Pour chicken broth into a large pot, add chicken and ginger, and simmer for 5 minutes. Add onion, celery, carrots, and mushrooms, and simmer another 4 to 5 minutes.

Drain long rice and cut into 3-inch lengths. Add long rice and green onions to the pot and stir. Cook an additional 5 minutes or until long rice becomes translucent.

ABOUT LONG RICE

Long rice, also known as bean threads or cellophane noodles, is made from mung beans. These are available in Chinese markets, and look like bundles of thin, hard translucent white noodles. Long rice has very little flavor of its own—but will easily absorb flavor of other ingredients. Once soaked, the noodles become soft and gelatinous. Take care not to overcook them—so they don't become mushy.

Pineapple Haupia

This simple but delicious pudding goes way back, to the days when the Hawaiians had only fruit, coconuts and wild sugar cane for sweets. I've given it a little twist by adding crushed pineapple.

Makes 12 servings

6 cups canned or fresh coconut milk
1 cup cornstarch
1 cup sugar
1/2 teaspoon salt
1 cup crushed pineapple

Drain pineapple, and squeeze out excess liquid and set aside.

Combine coconut milk, cornstarch, sugar and salt. Stir until cornstarch is dissolved. Cook on medium heat, stirring constantly, until it reaches the boiling point, then reduce heat to low. When it begins to thicken, add the pineapple and mix well.

Pour into individual dessert bowls, or sorbet glasses, and serve either warm or cold, topped with whipped cream. To serve cold, chill for at least 1 hour.

Tropical Drinks

Over the Rainbow

Loco Loco Mocha Mocha

Tropical Itch

Haupia with a Kick

Lava Flow

Guava Colada From the Valley

Kona Mac Freeze

Bermuda Triangle

You are the Bestest

Sam's North Shore Smoothie

Scorpion in a Glass

Over the Rainbow

1 ounce Malibu rum

2 ounces pineapple juice

2 ounces cranberry juice

1 ounce Midori liqueur

Ice

Garnish:

1/4 slice of pineapple

1 orchid

Fill hurricane glass with ice. Add ingredients. Float with 1 ounce of Midori liqueur, and garnish with 1/4 slice of pineapple and an orchid.

Loco Loco Mocha Mocha

Chocolate syrup

1 ounce Coco Rum

1 ounce Kahlua

1 ounce half and half

3 ounces pineapple juice

1 ounce Kahluaccino

Ice

Garnish:

3 tablespoons whipped cream

Cocoa Powder

1 maraschino cherry

Squirt chocolate syrup around the inside of a 14-ounce hurricane glass. Fill blender with ice to 1/3 full. Add ingredients, and blend until creamy.

Pour into hurricane glass, leaving 1/4-inch at the top. Cap with whipped cream, and dust with a little cocoa powder. Place cherry on whipped cream.

Tropical Itch

1 ounce orange Curacao
2 ounces orange juice
1 ounce Orgeat syrup
1 ounce dark rum
Ice

Garnish:
1/4 slice of pineapple
1 orchid
1 backscratcher (optional)

Fill blender with ice to 1/3 full. Add orange Curacao, orange juice and Orgeat syrup. Blend until slushy, and pour into hurricane glass. Float with dark rum, and garnish with 1/4 slice of pineapple, an orchid and a backscratcher!

Over the Rainbow, Loco Loco Mocha Mocha, Tropical Itch

Haupia with a Kick, "Oh Yeah!"

1 ounce light rum
2 ounces Coco Lopez coconut syrup
1 ounce half and half
Ice

Garnish:
1 orchid

Fill blender with ice to 1/3 full. Blend all ingredients, then pour into tall glass, and garnish with an orchid.

Lava Flow (Get it while it's hot!)

2 ounces strawberry purée
1 ounce light rum
1 ounce pineapple juice
1 ounce sweet & sour mix
1 ounce coconut syrup
1 ounce half and half
Ice
Garnish:
1/4 slice of pineapple
1 orchid

Pour strawberry purée into a 14-ounce hurricane glass. Fill blender with ice to 1/3 full, and add all other ingredients. Purée until slushy. Tilt hurricane glass to the side, and gently pour blender purée down the inside of the glass, careful not to disturb the strawberry purée.

Haupia with a Kick, Lava Flow, Guava Colada,
and Kona Mac Freeze

Guava Colada From the Valley

1 ounce light rum
1 ounce pineapple juice
2 ounces guava juice concentrate
1 ounce Coco Lopez coconut syrup
1 ounce half and half
Ice

Garnish:
1/4 of pineapple slice
1 orchid

Fill blender with ice to 1/3 full. Add ingredients, and blend until slushy. Pour into hurricane glass, and garnish with quarter of a pineapple slice and an orchid.

Kona Mac Freeze

1 ounce Kahlua
1 ounce Kahana Mac Nut Liqueur
1 ounce half and half
Ice

Garnish:
3 tablespoons whipped cream
1 teaspoon ground macadamia nuts

Fill blender with ice to 1/3 full. Add ingredients, and blend until creamy. Pour into a tall glass to 1/4-inch from the top. Add whipped cream, and sprinkle with ground macadamia nuts.

Bermuda Triangle

I ounce vodka

I ounce pineapple juice

I ounce orange juice

I ounce Grenadine syrup

I ounce sweet & sour mix

I ounce Midori liqueur

Ice

Garnish:

1/4 of a pineapple slice

I maraschino cherry

Fill hurricane glass with ice, then begin to build drink. Start with vodka, then add pineapple juice, orange juice, Grenadine, and top with sweet and sour. Float with Midori, or top with a pineapple slice (quartered) and a maraschino cherry.

You are the Bestest

1 ounce Kahlua
1 ounce Bailey's Irish Cream
1 ounce coconut syrup
1 ounce ripe banana
1 ounce half and half
Ice

Garnish:
1 slice of banana
1/4 slice of pineapple

Fill blender with ice to 1/3 full. Add ingredients, and blend until creamy. Pour mixture into tall glass, garnish with slice of banana, and 1/4 slice of pineapple.

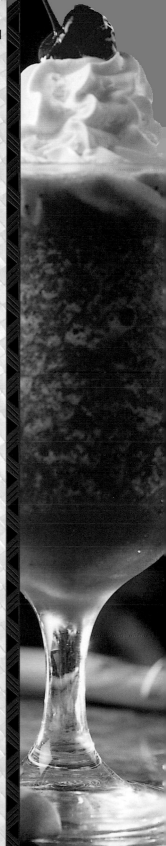

Bermuda Triangle, You are the Bestest, Sam's North Shor
Smoothie, and Scorpion in a Glass

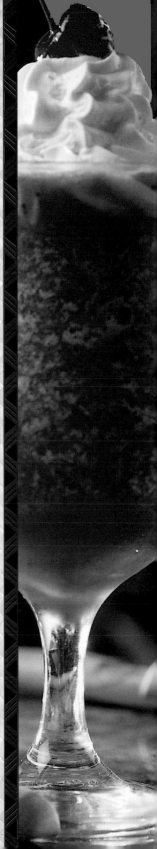

Sam's North Shore Smoothie

1 ounce vodka
1 ounce orange juice
1 ounce cranberry juice
2 ounces strawberry purée
1 ounce Grenadine syrup
Ice

Garnish:
3 tablespoons whipped cream
1 maraschino cherry

Fill blender with ice to 1/3 full. Add ingredients, and blend. Pour mixture into a tall glass, and top with whipped cream. Garnish with a maraschino cherry.

Scorpion in a Glass

1 ounce light rum
1 ounce brandy
2 ounces orange juice
1 ounce Orgeat syrup
Ice

Garnish:
1/2 slice of orange

Fill blender with ice to a little less than 1/4 full. Add ingredients, and blend. Pour mixture into a champagne flute, and garnish with slice of orange.

Glossary

'Ahi —Hawaiian name for yellowfin or bigeye tuna. Also called shibi in Japanese. When the term 'ahi is used in a recipe, it is assumed that fresh tuna, rather than canned, will be used.

Aku—the Hawaiian word for skipjack or bonito tuna. This fish is often eaten raw as an appetizer.

Al Dente—Italian phrase meaning to cook foods such as pasta and vegetables to the point where they still offer a slight resistance to the bite.

Asian Chili Sauce—this type of sauce is composed of chili peppers, vinegar, salt and sugar. Sriracha sauce is an example.

Bean Thread Noodles—a thin, clear noodle made from the starch of the mung bean. These relatively flavorless noodles soak up the flavors of other ingredients in a dish. They are also called cellophane noodles, and are known as long rice in Hawai'i.

Black Goma—see SESAME SEEDS.

Bok Choy—also known as pak choy or Chinese white cabbage. It has dark green leaves and long white stems, and can be purchased at Chinese markets.

Chicken Stock—as defined for the recipes in this book, it is assumed that the stock will be made without the addition of salt. If using a salted homemade or commercial broth, reduce salt in the recipe.

Chili Paste—a condiment composed of hot red chilies, vinegar, salt and sometimes garlic. Indonesian or Malay Sambal Oelek is an example.

Cilantro—leaves of the coriander plant. Also known as Chinese parsley.

Clarified Butter—golden liquid, which separates from unsalted butter when heated. It can be used for cooking at higher temperatures due to its higher smoke point. See recipe on page 3.

Coconut Milk—the liquid extracted by squeezing the grated meat of a coconut; most often found in canned and frozen forms. If you want to make it fresh, see recipe on page 78.

Coconut Syrup—a syrup, made from coconut milk and sugar, used for pancakes and tropical drinks.

Five Spice Powder—a spice blend generally consisting of ground cloves, fennel seeds, star anise, cinnamon and Szechwan pepper; used in Chinese and Vietnamese cuisines.

Ginger—the gnarled rhizome of a tall, flowering plant (Zingiber officinale) native to China. In Hawai'i, where it is grown, it is most frequently used fresh. Though also available powdered, pickled or candied, these forms are not good substitutes for fresh ginger.

Goma—see SESAME SEEDS.

Haupia—Hawaiian name given to coconut pudding, but now often used for many coconut-flavored desserts.

Hawaiian Chili Pepper—a very small (1/2 to 1 inch long) and extremely hot pepper, similar to the Caribbean bird chili.

Hawaiian Salt—white coarse sea salt.

'Inamona—Hawaiian word for a relish (in paste or chopped form) made from roasted kukui nuts and usually salt.

Julienne—to cut a food into thin strips similar in size to matchsticks.

Kukui Nuts—the Hawaiian name for the nuts of the candlenut tree; a main component of 'INAMONA.

Limu—Hawaiian word for all types of plants living in the water or damp places. The use of the word limu today generally applies to only edible seaweeds.

Limu Kohu—a highly prized edible red seaweed that may range in color from tan through shades of pink to dark red (Asparagopsis taxiformis).

Liquid Smoke—a basting or flavoring ingredient with an artificial smoky flavor and aroma. Found in the spice section of supermarkets.

Long Rice—translucent thread-like noodles made from mung bean flour. See BEAN THREAD NOODLES.

Lū'au Leaf—young taro leaves that must be cooked thoroughly 50-60 minutes before eating. Spinach makes an acceptable substitute.

Macadamia Nuts—rich, slightly sweet nuts that are a major crop in Hawai'i; often called "Mac Nuts."

Mahimahi—also called dolphinfish, but not related to the marine mammal; a mild-flavored, firm-fleshed fish.

Mango—a sweet and aromatic fruit that ranges in size from 1/4 to 2 pounds and tastes like a slightly resinous peach. Varieties range in color from greenish-yellow to red when ripe.

Maui Onions—large white onion noted for its sweet flavor, grown in Kula, the up-country region of Maui. Substitute with other sweet onions, such as Vidalia.

Mochiko—a flour made from glutinous rice with a high starch content. Available in Japanese markets.

Mustard Cabbage—a Chinese cabbage known for its pungency and slight bitterness; also known as kai choy and gai choy.

Napa Cabbage—also known as celery cabbage, Chinese cabbage and won bok. Pale green at the top to white at the stem with crinkly leaves.

Ogo—also limu manauea, the type of seaweed most commonly referred to in Hawai'i simply as "limu." Color can range from green to reddish-brown; its filaments have a crisp texture and a mild flavor. *(Gracilaria coronopifolia* and *Gracilaria bursapastoris)*

Ono—a type of fish also called wahoo; a member of the mackerel family. Grouper, snapper or sea bass can be substituted.

'Opakapaka—Hawaiian name for the pink or crimson snapper.

Oyster Sauce—a concentrated dark-brown sauce made from oysters, salt and soy sauce. Used in many Asian dishes to impart a full, rich flavor.

Panko—Japanese-style breadcrumbs, coarser than regular breadcrumbs. Substitute with regular unseasoned dry breadcrumbs.

Papaya—in Hawai'i this sweet, yellow, pear-shaped fruit is about 6 to 10 inches long. A common size will yield about 1-1/2 to 2 cups flesh.

Poha—Hawaiian word for the cape gooseberry; also known as golden berry or ground cherry. The yellow, marble-sized fruit hangs on the plant inside a lantern-shaped, paper-like husk.

Poi—Hawaiian word for a dish made of cooked taro pounded to a paste with the addition of water. It must be a consistency that allows it to be consumed with one, two or three fingers.

Poke—Hawaiian word meaning to slice or to cut into small bite-size pieces; refers to a traditional Hawaiian dish of raw seafood, fresh seaweed, Hawaiian salt and Hawaiian red chili peppers.

Portuguese Sausage—pork sausage with spicing that ranges from mild to hot. Italian sausage or other garlic sausage may be substituted if necessary.

Pupu—Hawaiian word meaning appetizer or snack to go with drinks.

Rice Vinegar—a type of vinegar made from rice wine; generally clear with a pale straw color. Generally, rice vinegar is mellow and lower in acid than other vinegars.

Sambal Oelek—see CHILI PASTE.

Sesame Oil—oil pressed from the sesame seed is available in two forms. Pressing the raw seed produces an oil, which is light in color and flavor and can be used for a wide variety of purposes. When the oil is pressed from toasted sesame seeds, it is dark in color with a much stronger flavor. It is this darker version that is to be used in the recipes of this book.

Sesame Seeds—the edible seeds of a plant of the Pedaliaceae family that have a distinctive nutty flavor. They come in black or white varieties, and are known as benne seeds and goma.

Shallot—this member of the onion family forms a bulb more like a garlic bulb and has a subtler flavor than green onions.

Shiitake Mushrooms—mushrooms native to Japan that are now cultivated in the Untied States; have tough stems that are not eaten and dark brown caps that have a meaty, smoky flavor. Dried shiitake need to be soaked in warm water until soft (20 to 30 minutes). Also called black Chinese mushrooms and golden oak mushrooms.

Snow Peas—young peas with edible pods consumed when the pods are thin and the seeds are still tiny.

Soy Sauce—a sauce made from fermented boiled soybeans and roasted wheat or barley; its color ranges from light or dark brown and its flavor is generally rich and salty. Used extensively in Chinese and Japanese cuisines as a flavoring, condiment and a cooking medium.

Taro—Tahitian word for a starchy tuber that can be baked or boiled like potatoes or pounded into a paste called poi. The large green taro leaves can be eaten, but must be cooked thoroughly to remove oxalic acid crystals, which cause a prickly sensation in the throat. Cooked spinach can be substituted for cooked taro leaf.

Teriyaki—a Japanese broiling technique that uses a soy sauce-based glaze to season meat or fish.

Ti Leaf—long, slender leaf most easily recognizable from their use in hula skirts. They are used to wrap a variety of foods for cooking. The leaves are not consumed.

Tofu—Japanese name for a bland soy bean curd that can be custard-like in texture or quite firm. The firm or extra firm varieties are generally used in stir-frying or deep-frying.

Wasabi—also called Japanese horseradish; comes in both powder and paste forms. It is pale green in color, and produces a sharp, tingling sensation in the nose and palate.

Wok—a round or flat-bottomed Chinese cooking pan used for stir-frying or deep-frying foods.

Won Ton Wrappers—very thin sheets of wheat flour and egg dough typically used to make Chinese dumplings. Wrappers come in 3-1/2-inch squares and 7-inch squares. They may be cut into strips and fried, and used like croutons.

Ingredient Source Guide

The following are a few telephone and Internet sources for ingredients that are difficult to obtain outside of Hawai'i. Some of the sources have retail outlets you can visit—the addresses are given below.

Hawaii Seafood Express

This source is an Internet shopping site that offers fresh Hawaiian seafood such as 'ahi, 'opakapaka and mahimahi. Also offered are ogo, limu kohu, Hawaiian salt and poi. Website: http://www.hawaiiseafoodexpress.com

The Hawaii Store

Located in San Francisco, this retail and telephone source has a wide range of Hawaiian merchandise, including hard-to-find items like frozen lū'au leaves.

The Hawaii Store
2655 Judah Street • San Francisco, CA 94122
Telephone: 1 (877) 4HOWZIT
Email: THStore@aol.com

Sun Jose Hawaii

The largest source of Hawaiian products in Northern California.

Sun Jose Hawaii
410 West Capitol Expressway and Vista Park Drive • San Jose, CA 95136
Telephone: 1 (877) 786-5673
Website: http://www. sunjose.com
Email: sunjose@aol.com

Takahashi Market

A source for Panko breadcrumbs, limu, salt salmon, fresh poi, 'inamona and Hawaiian salt.

Takahashi Market
221 South Claremont Street • San Mateo, CA 94401
Telephone: (650) 343-0394
Website: http://www.menehune.com/takahashi
Email: tmarket@aol.com

Index

Notes

_____

_____

_____

_____

_____

_____

_____

_____

_____

_____

_____

_____

_____

_____

_____

_____

_____

_____

_____